salmonpoetry

Her Father's Daughter

Nessa O'Mahony

Published in 2014 by
Salmon Poetry
Cliffs of Moher, County Clare, Ireland
Website: www.salmonpoetry.com
Email: info@salmonpoetry.com

ISBN 978-1-908836-85-4

COVER IMAGE: *The collection of Keith Haynes and the McCann family*
COVER DESIGN & TYPESETTING: *Siobhán Hutson*
Printed in Ireland by Sprint Print

Salmon Poetry gratefully acknowledges the support of
The Arts Council / An Chomhairle Ealaoín

For Peter Salisbury
with love
and
in memory of my father
Donal J. O'Mahony
(1926-2010)

Acknowledgments

I would like to thank the Board and staff of the Djerassi Resident Artists Program at Woodside, California, where some of these poems were completed during a month's residency there in July 2005; thanks, too, to the Tyrone Guthrie Centre in Annaghmakerrig, Co. Monaghan, for the bursary that sent me to California.

I'm grateful to former teachers and colleagues at Bangor University, North Wales, who truly made me feel I had a home from home between 2003 and 2006. I am particularly grateful to South Dublin County Council and An Chomhairle Éalaíon / The Arts Council for their generous financial assistance during the final stages of completing this manuscript. Finally, thanks to Marianne Jones, Tan Morgan, Lorna Sherry and John O'Donoghue for their astute and generous critique of some of the poems included here, and to Eabhan Ni Shuillebháin and Noel Duffy for their wise feedback on the final draft.

I am grateful to the editors of the following magazines and journals where some of these poems have appeared: *Aesthetica, Agenda, The Black Mountain Review, Breaking The Skin, Crannóg, Eire-Ireland, The Irish Times, New Writing, Orbis, Nth Position, Poetry Ireland Review, Sand, Southword, The Shop a Magazine of Poetry, The Stinging Fly, Van Gogh's Ear* and *Ygdragsil*.

Contents

I

II

III

IV

V

I

Giving Me Away

Because you had never walked me down the aisle
you sit 330 miles in the passenger seat,
watching the speed-dial, miming brakes
when the arrow climbs too high for your liking.

Britain speeds by, an AA list
of pubs and service stations,
place-names striking chords, fuelling
small-talk about battle sites and pit-stops.

We stop at a Little Chef,
debate if one of us should wait
to mind the car's contents;
I let you win, this time.

By Birmingham I realise we've never spent
so long in each other's company.
Which might explain
why you don't always reply,

seem lost in maps,
worried by junction numbers,
ask me to repeat myself so often
that I snap my irritation back at you.

On we drive, each mile a little closer
to my new start, my resolve lasting
until you ask me for the umpteenth
what it was that I just said

and I know you've already
left me on this trip,
at Holyhead, at Dublin Port
before the ship embarked.

In the Years Before Sex

I knitted,
strange, lovely yarns,
russet-flecked,
rare indigoes.
I plained and purled,
needles clicking
to their own speed,
clicking each tick
of the clock,
length, breadth-ways.

I didn't have to look,
could gaze rapt
at fire flames
while it grew and grew
till it was a river
breaking its banks,
tumbling out,
and the whole floor
was swamped.
I knitted
intricacies:
Aran crosses,
fisherman's rib,
blackberry,
garter and loops,
moss, seed stitch,
open honeycomb,
making sure
the seams obeyed

and I knitted
scarlets, blues,
I knitted
to be useful,
until my fingers
ached, the knuckles
forcing through
bruised skin
against the bones
clicking their steady click,
inexorable,
not letting me slow
down.

I knitted
till the last ball
unwound
to a small curl
spiralling
the air.

Madam Butterfly at Beaumaris

Tonight I observe the old rituals,
run a warm bath, descend,
soak, sponge, massage each limb,
let the heat enter me.
After, I'm gentle when I rub myself down,
anoint with oil of cocoa butter,
finger-tip smooth cream in elbow folds,
around each breast, caress
the waist sloping to buttock rise.
I go to the window seat,
kimono loose-wrapped, hair unpinned.
All is readiness; Callas sings,
a red buoy light flashes my intentions to the Straits.
I wait for tomorrow
when you said you'd come.

Doorways

Your first shot,
me framed in the door
of my grandmother's house
in Garbally.

Our first stay,
and it feels strange when
I'm trusted with the key,
with instructions
on how to keep the fire lit.

You mention
Granny's house
and it sounds alien
on your lips;
she was dead years
before I met you.

But she always predicted
the old sock would find
the old shoe

eventually.

Sibyl at the Rockefeller

She is a strange choice for guide,
this four foot, 70-plus, dryad of skyscrapers.
Powder chaotically applied,
feather boa, red shoes, more suited
to the Rainbow Room 65 floors up
than this rain-dashed sidewalk.

Like her sister in the Harbour,
she grasps her book of truth
but relies on memory it seems;
she was the small child gazing up
as men ate sandwiches mid-air,
resting on tight-roped steel.
The Irish (and the Indians)
had the best heads for height.

She leads us, voice magnified through earphones
thoughtfully supplied at the desk.
Her constant injunction *Don't look back, look up*
at machine-cut design, the glory
of chrome escalators, art deco sunburst elevators,
tiger's eye in black marble.

She intones her litany:
the ambition of Junior, of Hood,
the vision of Lee Lawrie and Brangwyn;
we tut at the crimes of Diego Rivera,
then come to a halt behind Atlas,
look through his legs at the Gothic
dropped-out-of-the-sky squat of St Pats,
attempt to spot the familiar
in the bent frame, arms transfixed.
Others have guessed wrong
(Batman, the Terminator);
she approves as you conjure Christ
from tortured limbs.

We paid for an hour;
she gives us 90 minutes
before a startled glance,
a shy exchange of tips –
my five dollar bill outdone by her
Go to the river, the only way
to see the place is from water –
and she's gone, her minute form drowned
by crowds swimming upstream.

"Surprised by joy"

ambushed by sunlight
and birdsong.

A moment's work,
the time it took
to connect a call,
hear a flat tone.

Hair's breadth between
light and shade,
what we hold,
what we give away
or have taken from us.

And if we retrieve,
can we hold cleanly
a child's faith

that the sun will always rise,
the blackbird sing.

His Master's Voice

In memory of James Simmons

Charlie hasn't heard it for a while.
The world's gone quiet, his milk-skin eyes
see shadows mostly, nothing to make him rise
in greeting, tail wagging stiffly.

There's been a change,
the house full suddenly,
people blundering around,
treading on his tail.

Now the room is empty,
the bed made, the coffin
carried out.

They'd stood around it
earlier, lips moving.
He'd felt the rumble of a lorry
passing by and barked.

In the morning, he lets his nose direct him,
past the sour-sweet smells
on table-tops, the tang of dripping cans
and empty whiskey bottles,
to the patio where a refuse sack lies,
shredded by night-time predators.

Contents strewn,
he quickly finds the scent;
his master's slippers, night-gown,
the smell of sweat still clinging.

He can't know that a stranger
will come soon, tidying,
sweeping up, thieving a poem
like a starving cur grabs a bone
where she finds it.

Portrait of the Artist's Father

Years ago when I was young
and hadn't lost anyone
I wrote about a sketch a poet made
of his dying mother.
My words were cool, disapproving:
those tidy coal-strokes of the dead

Now, what else can I do
as I sit and watch you sleep
one of your countless
dress rehearsals?
Eyes shut but darting constantly,
lids pulsing with each twitch
as you fight the demon of the hour.

I trawl for metaphors,
imagine corollaries
for the fluid filling your lungs,
some dark assailant
emerging from the shade,
hands flexed.

Your mouth works wordlessly,
offers no clues.
You may be reading from another script,
borrowed, perhaps, from the novel
you've taken weeks to read.

My page
has been empty
for months.
Forgive me
for filling it.

Those Of Us Left

Three of us here,
four if you count the collie dog
you didn't meet though heard about
the last time we spoke;
you laughed
at my cosy domesticity,
compared notes on dust,
on box unpacking,
made plans for the weekend.

Those of us left
can't plan yet,
can barely put
one foot
in front of the other
though the pressure
on the leash,
an animal's hunger
for strange sights and smells,
reminds us that we must.

I grapple your lover's grief,
try to stifle the anger
that rises in waves.
It might help
if I knew who to target:
the you in that box?
Or me?
The stone I kick
into the river?

Tibradden Mountain

Start with what you know,
with what you were told.

You cannot step into
the same stream twice,
the water has muddied,
cleared, then browned again
with debris of the past.
The glimpse you catch,
the refraction of face,
too fleeting to recognise.

But what of this room,
these four walls,
the view of the garden
you planted when you thought
your roots were buried here?

The crab-apple
has thrived
in your absence,
its autumn load
clustering,
embarrassing
robins and firecrests
with riches.

What of
the wider world?
Don't look there
for points of reference;
Dublin's new tale,
writ large
in wood and stone,
endless queues
for motorways.

Look up, then.
The hills have
the same contours:
Killakee Wood
all short, back and sides,
the toothy gap
for the grey threat
of Hellfire.

To the left,
the Pine Forest
blankets Tibradden.
Its gentle slopes
a lure on Sunday mornings.

Room for us all:
sulky scouts
hunting in packs,
the well-prepared
with their maps
and waterproofs.

The path forks.
You follow
the river bed,
a stream still
after the dry summer.
You baulk
at the treachery
of wet rock.

At the top,
a jagged crop,
the rusted sign
announcing
you are in a place
once thought holy.

Below, the Dublin plains
compete with
grey clouds
and wind.

To your right,
the cairn at Two Rock
beaconing back,
to your left
the Hellfire Club
like a granite bead
in this rosary.

You stand
in the heart,
stare at the carved slab,
concentric spirals
etched 2000 years ago,
or only 200.
The stream has changed,
the message the same,
though.

Late Spring

For Peter

It has kept us waiting: branches bare,
tiny buds compact with withheld promise
as we huddle in winter-gear, look sunward
for the green on frosted hills.
Birds probe soil with sceptical bills;
claws tap worm-morse; little stirs.

Sunlight oblique through windows,
catches dust of jobs still to be done,
catches the corner of a wedding photograph
not yet six months old. The couple smiling
in their Autumn-best, lisianthus grasped
in remembrance of the decades missed,
trusting that seasons shift,
that movement is always forward.

II

St Brigid's Day, Woodside Road, Norwich

For Fiona Curran

It's just as well we didn't bet our souls on it.
This first day of pagan spring dawns white,
the two-day fall blanking out pavements,
children making hay of it with snowballs.
One attempts, Sisyphus-like, to roll a boulder heavier
than his bodyweight up the embankment.
Mothers in tracksuits supervise from front-doors,
fathers, scrapers in hand, track warily round cars.
Sane people stay indoors, waiting for the equinox
and the met office to make it official.
But I brave the frost, looking for some augury or other,
find it in a melted six inch square in Violet's planter.
I hunker down for a closer look, then bow before
green shoots tangled in a perfect plaited cross.

February Vase

It takes
the whole day;
an oh so slow
opening up,
loosening
yellow stays,
stems bending
beneath the weight
of corona.

Drawn
towards light,
a choice
between rain-lashed
spattered glass
and a source
closer to home.
They turn,
opening full lips
to lamp light.

Harbinger

Elsewhere it's swallows.
Here it's the first boats,
filing a course through the Straits,
leaning against the wind,
testing sails that haven't been
unfurled for months.

I follow each craft
through the span
of my bay window,
imagine the rest,
the progress past the pier,
white cloth reflected
in each pane of glass
of the seafront terrace.
It curves its way
towards Penmon and the light.

Another, anchored
unseen overnight,
circles on its moorings
as the wind shifts.

Aillwee

300 metres down,
so deep
that drips grow.

We stop
where the guide
places us,
admire the bear pits,
the mineral sheen
on walls,
how cathode
lights the stream,
quick silver falling.

In the halogen glow
we nearly miss
the one small
green frond
sprouting from
a ledge above,
chlorophyll
vivid against
grey wall.

The guide
disapproves,
explains
the science
of spores
falling through
grikes,
of timer lights
that simulate
the god-given.

He would
eradicate;
we demur,
taking our miracles
where we find them.

Natural Selection

After scanning "The Movements and Habits of Climbing Plants"
by Charles Darwin, MRA, FRS, John Murray, Abermarle Street, 1875

April blusters into May,
plays a glassy tune
on the wind chimes
guarding the crab-apple
from bull-finch rapine.

At my desk on the first floor,
I miss most of the garden-action,
though the upward climb
of pink and white
on the silver birch
can still arrest me.

Each year a yard more
up the green cascade;
the tree's delicate limbs
can't withstand
the steady upward creep
of clematis Montana,
the sinuous grip
of passion-flower.

The white twines higher
than its pink-tipped mate,
blossoms lighter,
lured on by cloud,
evolved enough to ignore
the pull of gravity.

The manuals frown
on this symbiosis;
I applaud
the subtle strength
of tendril,
the ruthlessness of vine.

Year of the Rat

I live with your
scrambling
between walls,
scratching pipes
in early morning.

Things shift,
dart too fast
for the blink of my eye.
You leave a trace,
small but intact.

I taste your quickness,
smell your sloped back,
the bone easing under
doors, through cracks
in woodwork.

Holes are the enemy,
wire wool-barbed
in the no-man's land
between fridge and wall.

Soon you will win
the kitchen floor, the hall,
the landing. Four walls
unhoming me
as you claim your own.

Visitor

A garden with a mouse in it
is a shape-shifting place;
a space of quick darts,
of dashes round plant pots,
courage snatched with birdseed.

It is a word hovering
out of reach, an image
half seen, a notion half-
realised, the perfect line
diffusing into vapour.

Seagull

A call, softer
than the raucous chorus I've got used to.
I seek the source, my eye takes time
to spot the skylight perch
of twigs and moss and pier debris.

She sits, occasionally nods at her mate
who's now the sole provider.
He takes off, flies over signs that warn
of penalties should someone feed him.
She plucks at bedding,
discards rolling down to guttering.

At night, she's a grey against tiles.

Neither of us can know her time is short,
that the van will come soon, the men
emerging with ladders and sacks
they'll carry up, smashing
the carefully assembled bed,
sky white with screeching.

The woman in the hairdressers says
a panther's prowling the woods
round Henllys; maiming calves, she says.
I tell her: death stalks closer than that.

Hawks

They circle the ridge,
loops widening,
narrowing,
swooping low,
two shadows inscribe
two arcs on singed grass.

They seem choreographed,
dancers mirroring
their story in curves,
rotating round
without intersection,

like you, arms stretched,
hands curling like
a supplicant's,
or me, the marionette
bobbing my head
as I tell my story,

you, yours,
wide-limbed,
using all the stage,

me on
the one
spot,
turning
my tight
curve.

Environmental Enhancement Scheme, Galway City

A day of half-light, a tang of salt in the air,
a wind that chastens stragglers into perpetual motion
in this maze of streets, worm casts of the old city.

We raise our collars to nose level,
find Nun's Island across bridges that bring us there,
return us later to somewhere only half familiar.

By now the sun is a pale disc wrapped in tissue
so we keep our jackets on, come to the canal,
a washed-out strip, emptied of juices.

A group of tourists lean over the wall,
gaze fixedly into the sludge
of the drained-off bed.

We follow their stare,
curious at what holds them
among old tyres and pop-eyed cans,

till we see it, a sliver of light,
a black, serpentine curl
as it bores through mud,

trying to retrieve the elements
it swam between
before its world reversed.

It tunnels on, slow painful slog
as the ticking dial undrapes itself,
drying the bed out, cracking stones.

Further on, the casual wall-top shape
of a heron, all lacy neck and sharp glance,
taking his time, measuring his chances.

Snake Tale

for Skip Gianocca

The fourth-generation mountain man
carries the garbage can to the deck,
lid roped tight by a frayed bicycle cord.

A broom is brought, wand for the magic trick
but there's no rabbit here,
unless one swallowed earlier.

Lid removed, he shakes the can,
bangs the interior with the stick, receives
the requisite response, rattle, though no hiss.

Lozenge head, diamond skin, although
not Ouroboros now and I'm wishing
this sad coil would exert itself,

insinuate up the rod and into symbol.
But this is fact: trapped by the rubber base
of a garbage can.

The man shows his prize possession,
the amulet of five rattles,
corn-husk light:

bound by a silver bird,
a turquoise-eyed phoenix
promising resurrections of a kind.

III

Her Father's Daughter

The first time I know:
standing hip-high to her
as she lifts the receiver
of the old black phone
in the dining room.

She must have cried before
but I've never seen it,
never made the link
between my garden falls
and these grown-up trails
of moisture on her cheeks.
On mine, the rough feel
of tweed, the pressure
of knees I cling to
as her hand goes to lips,
hides a silent 'oh'
like air escaping.

She'll make that sound
40 years later,
in the corridor of a hospital ward
when she hears that her man
died without her.

Right now we're innocent
of patterning;
she's left the confines
of a suburban dining room,
is hearing the tale
of how her dad threw his head back,
laughed his last

and I'm clinging on tighter.
Perhaps she releases me,
perhaps someone else takes my hand
and guides me to where
I'll wait out this mystery.

Casting Lots

I

History doesn't record
how you decided it:
the flip
of a thrupenny bit,
a card, a straw,
in an unnamed pub
somewhere
in the English midlands.
You'd never mistake
those grey tufts
for Derryronane.

I doubt a white feather
was behind it;
more like you'd caught
a thirst,
the American liner stub
still in your pocket.
History does record
the outward journey
(SS Baltic, from Queenstown
27th June, 1913)
you may have swum back

just in time
to have a pint
with the brother
and decide who'd go,
who'd return
to farm and family.

I try to picture the pair:
two young broths,
shoulders hunched
at the bar,
a tolerant English hand
serving stout
(it would become
a life-long devotion)
high cheekbones,
pale blue eyes
weighing the future up.

II

Family lore is mute
on where or when you got yourself
photographed,
kitted out as the pride
of the Munster Fusiliers
(your granddaughter
omits the Royal —
did your tongue elide it?)

Like a child
from a dress-up box
with your wide belt
and your peaked cap,
though the shaved head
is a clue to the war game
you're playing.
Your right hand holds a cane,
as if the photographer guessed
the future legacy.

Family legend is mute
on when you sent it.
I'm picturing it in slow-motion,
an envelope spiralling down
like a chicken's feather,
a scurry from the back
to gather it up.
Did it have pride of place
on a mantelpiece?
Did your mother
turn a leaf
of the family bible,
position you face down
on the Book of Joshua?

Church Hill, Ballinasloe

In your wake again, Mother,
heading down Dunloe Street,
chasing another tale.

You're an expert guide,
though it's sixty-five years
since you last came home here.

We've been by the Barracks,
your father traced in accounts
of parades and drills and emergencies.

The decades drop away,
the bold child reappears as we climb
the former Victoria Avenue.

I picture the unruly troupe
of boys and girls, blonde, blue-eyed,
the devil in the detail

that your plain clothes D.I. father
couldn't talk down from trees
round Clancarty's monument.

At the top of the hill,
the Protestant church
looks ancient, venerable,

though appearances deceive.
A fire burnt it out (friend or foe?),
it would have been just rebuilt

when you jostled for views
of the gentry en route for service,
then raced past the alms house

to the wall just by the door
to line up in order of height
and await inspection.

We arrive. You haven't been inside
since 1945 though your dreams
have brought you back constantly.

An office-refit cannot disguise:
the tall stairs reshape into a slide
for nine brothers and sisters;

back bedroom re-arranges
into dormitory, then sick-room;
the window, deep-set, at the front

with a view to the clock-tower;
that the view's now blocked
doesn't seem to bother you.

I envy you this, Mother.
I envy the clear sight, the instant recall,
the glimpses of all that prelapsarian joy.

Walking Stick

An honest thing:
ash shaft, plain,
crook smooth,
no gentleman's cane
of silver or amethyst tip,
of snakewood.

Crafted to bear weight,
the tonnage of trench-foot,
splintered bones, toe lost
in the ambush at Glore
(another conflict,
the same cost).

Shoved to the side,
or brandished as threat
for the boys' *divilment*;
they used bullets as toys,
did you silently smile
as they echoed you?

Needed more each year,
then daily once another war,
our *Emergency*, broke out
and you drilled the boys
from the town to defend the realm
against farmers' sons.

Decommissioned once again
into night-watchman jobs
in Coventry, in Cricklewood.
You still looked tough, the stick
found a hook in boarding houses;
you'd only take it out after hours.

It came to our house when you died,
spent decades under the stairs
till you daughter needed it,
trimmed it down to size.
A match for mine. I heft it up:
it still bears its weight.

Role Reversal

after Eavan Boland

There will come a time, mother,
when the transformed spring opens up
and the charioteer holds out a hand;
he might have my father's face, might not;
his gestures might be gentle or rough
as he eases you into a space made ready
and shows you the pomegranate.
And you will take the seed and eat,
willingly perhaps, not caring
that every bargain has its cost,
or will your hand be stayed
by the sun's ray on your face?
I will not have time to catch up,
to forestall the nine long days,
the nine long nights of wandering.
And I'll have no deal to strike;
no backward glance, no waiting
for the seasons to turn back to me.

IV

Waiting Room

The rules for survival:
don't catch an eye
on the first day,
look away
if their blank grief
grazes over you.

If still here the next,
permit a faint smile,
a nod to a fellow traveller.
But keep your space,
don't approach
unless invited
and only then
with care.

Avoid those
with a story to tell,
a need to eat you alive
as they rave
about hands squeezed,
the twitch of a closed eye.

You can't spare
a shred, a prayer;
it's dog eat dog here.
The odds are too high,
if somebody has to die,
let the noose swing
elsewhere.

No News Is Good News

The sun has returned,
drawing me out
to the seafront where you'd take
your constitutional.

The last time you came here
I was three thousand miles away.
I had to imagine your promenade
down the pier, then your choice:
left for the cliff walk,
right to Gallows Point.

Just names, then,
innocent of intent.

Now, sixty plus nautical miles
from where you lie
in your hospital bed,
the wind whips up,
gives excuse for the tears
that spring unaccountably often,
though there's no threat,
they tell me.

No news is good news, I'm told.
And like a bold child
I feel cheated
that I must wait here
to check the phone for messages,
take my place in the queue
for family updates,
cling to each sign of progress
relayed long distance,
a tube removed,
an improved gulp
promising food.

Strange days.

Did I ever tell you that once,
back home in Churchtown,
glancing round your door
to say goodnight,
I caught your bowed back,
your bent knees,
a 78-year-old
Christopher Robin?

I crept out,
embarrassed.

Last night
I knelt by my bed,
joined my hands,
bowed my head,
said the words
you taught me
four decades ago,
though the order
may have been wrong
and the list of the dead
lengthened.

The Long Goodbye

It has been a year
since you left
the hospital whites,
and were swallowed up
by your own chair
at the fire
we haven't lit
for years.

You've gradually
filled out,
reasserted your
grip of space,
of the remote control,
sprawl now like you own
the joint (and you still do).

Perhaps you don't need
the iron rail on the stair,
perhaps you do;
when I follow you up
I refuse
to notice.

Will it be this
I remember,
a swooped kiss
on your head
as you sit before
the computer screen
that baffles you
more than ever?

Or scattered images,
cine-camera jerked,
of the heart-throb,
younger you
out the back,
or on a Sunday walk
when Dodder Park
never looked lovelier?

Accident & Emergency

That is no country for old men;
the young get sloshed
and stagger through double doors,
tattoos on their arms,
eyes stoned.

The old men wait,
knowing their turn
is a moveable feast
despite the bluecoat's promises
they are eighth on the list.

And still they wait,
observe the to and fro,
the quick dispatch
of those who arrived
much later than they,
assess whose recovery
would seem the better bet.

Day crawls into night,
the digital clock
a silent mockery
(you'd need a calendar in here),
names called,
anyone's but theirs.

Glued to wheelchairs,
their motions
at the whim
of orderlies.

The old men wait;
they know they have no choice.
It has been ordained
by those who perhaps forget
how time passes.

Deserted Village, Achill Island

in memory of my father

A gap between showers,
blue filtering half-light,
so we take our chances
on the slopes of Slievemore.

Those who'd called it home
knew about impermanence,
the reach of bog,
the gaping sockets of roofs.

Hap-hazarding lazy beds,
slip-slides of water
pouring down
the side of the mountain,
we settle for the track,
the safety of shale and quartz.

Sun wets white shards,
crystal lures us
as the track forks
to where a burnt-out digger
acts sentinel over oil slicks;
wind chimes music:
a plastic bottle
trapped by bog-*lethe*.

The quarry opens out,
slag-heaps improbably white,
as if someone had cleared snow
into neat piles,
or had scattered detergent
like there was no tomorrow,
no white sheets to be spread out,
no single rose bud to be left
beside a hospital bed.

Invisible Monument

In a town square in Germany
an artist lifts 300 cobblestones.
Over a year he etches,
one by one, with painstaking care
the name that attached
some soul to flesh, to bones
that were rendered later
by fellow countrymen.

When done, he replaces
each face down
so the inscription is hidden,
and feet can step unaware
as footfall presses the name
deeper into the earth it sprang from.

We had one stone
carved with a name and a date
and a wishing;
planted it wind-ward.

Is it better, that facing up,
than memory that shifts shape,
reduces dimensions
to whatever fraction
the wind will weather?

Notes for an Exhibit

Spotfin Porcupine Fish, Cuba 1991,
D.J. O'Mahony, MI31.1992

It catches the eye:
half globe, half water-mine,
outrage suspended
in display case 781 *Vertebrata Pisces*
on the first floor landing.

When threatened, it doubles in size,
swallows air and water, bristles spines,
sends neurotoxins till each tip sizzles
with venom more potent than cyanide.

Still netted all the same,
(there is no armour against fate)
transformed to artefact,
presented in great state
to one who'd done some service.

What else need we know?
That it spent a year
atop a china cabinet,
caught dust, snagged cloth?
That it was the extra guest
at many a family party?
That, seeing it encased,
a grandson made an excited phone-call?

A six-inch black-type card
acknowledges the donor
of whom little is known;
his dates are found elsewhere.

V

Windfall

A crab's shell, belly-up
on a Clare beach,
expertly excavated
by a probing beak.

Did some alchemy of July air
paint the inner skin
such a delicate lavender?

A month later, the copse walk
at the back of Brookwood
is littered with chestnut shells,
prey to unseasonal winds.

Unopened,
the plump green promise
of mahogany.
Open, they are
blanched satin,
casketing a bullock's
albino eye.

Last night, four days
after your 46th birthday,
they planted a tree for you
on the hill at Killiney.

Red oak,
as slim and tall
as you stood
the last time
we saw you.

Niyma

for Debbie

The cat named for the sun
stretches on the deck,
narrows her eyes in the rays
of her foster mother,
feigns relaxed as
birds whirr around her.

A humming bird
comes close,
suspending judgement
in perpetual motion.

The cat
tenses her length,
assesses the gap
between reach
and aspiration.

The bird vibrates away.
The cat unwinds, descends
to better hunting grounds.

California Dreaming

On the deck in the dark,
trying to see through air
thick with dusk and mites
and stars that may be aliens.

Beneath, the undergrowth
rustles, moving
as if there were a breath
in this July heat.

We guess the source
by the weight of the noise:
too big to be mice,
you speculate raccoon.

I think of Davy Crockett.

I bought his hat
in a store that sold
saddles and chicks
and socks for horses,
where a stuffed coyote
leered from a wall.

The hat was
made in China.

Here, nothing comes
from its place,
unless perhaps
the white shapes we saw
darting through night,
fleet and pale and dog-like.

We test the air,
wait for more than
tall thistles moving
where there is
no wind.

After noon

Adam is nearly five.
He's singing next door,
notes scaling the fence,
stringing words half-heard
from a radio into endless lines
that swoop and dive to a tune
only he's sure of.

I strain to make sense of it,
the effort too great
as I sit in my doorframe,
watching the breeze tease
the montbretia.

Bennie slinks in,
the morning's mousing feat
a distant memory
as he winds himself
around my legs,
cocking an ear
for the scratch
he knows I'll offer.

And I watch the sky,
cloudless for once
in this Irish summer,
and think that
for the first time in a while,
I know how this could be
even more

perfect.

A Lesson in Politics
at the Bird Feeder

A chaffinch, sleekly pink,
autumn plumes fluffed
in the light breeze
of mid-October,
politely waits his turn
at the bird feeder.

He straddles a crab-apple,
benign, as a plethora
of smaller birds,
tits (Great, Coal),
even a Goldcrest,
do peck and grab runs
at the plastic-dome.

His patience pays off;
he takes his turn
and his fill
of seeds and grated nuts,
beak magisterial
and efficient
mid the spray
of grain and husks.
He retires
to a higher branch
to swallow.

In the pause
his mate arrives,
dull brown and buff,
tentative
at the plastic grill.
One peck is all

she gets.
The male descends,
chest puffed up,
song shrill
as he wings her off
the pedestal.

Feast of the Epiphany

The weather contrives
a white page on which
primary colours startle.
A bullfinch all blush-pink
on the hedge by the river,
redwings erupt
in browns and rust
from the forest floor.
A magpie swoops and dives
by my office window,
mistaking snowflakes
for the nutrients
she's desperate for.
My eye is perpetually drawn
from a white, flickering box
to a whiter screen
that might just erase
all sins, all memories:
false promising
fresh starts.

There Is Special Providence ...

A scatter of feathers the only sign
of a small murder.
My birder's guide can't identify
the forensics of blues and greys,
although a zoologist might guess
from the pentagonal cartilage joint,
mantilla spread on the path
behind the treefern.
I'd meant to be kind;
left feeders at either end,
the dog as guard;
he must have slept through it,
lips twitching a dream chase,
whimpers drowning out
the real thing.

Shortfall from the Perfect

After Helen O'Leary

One step
between earth
and water;
leaf-carpet
parts,
freeze-frame,
a dog paddles
to shore,
shakes,
shrugs off
sooner
than I can.
World is suddener *
and all that.
Give me
the certainty
of margins;
liminality
certainly
lacks.

* 'World is suddener than we think it is',
from Louis MacNeice's poem 'Snow'.

Murmuration at Six O'Clock

Seurat could have captured this,
the swarm and pulse
of a thousand starlings
over St. Peter's Basilica
as the light dips and the rain-tipped
Roman sky stains mulberry.
As far as the eye scans, birds rise
in ventricled waves
of fibonacci spirals,
gulls joining in, crows,
the parakeets from the Borghese,
till the air fills and bells
in each campanile sound
for every vespered swerve.

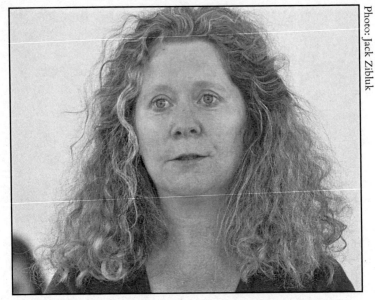

NESSA O'MAHONY was born in Dublin and lives in Rathfarnham where she works as a freelance teacher and writer. Her poetry has appeared in a number of Irish, UK, and North American periodicals and has been translated into several European languages. She won the National Women's Poetry Competition in 1997 and was shortlisted for the Patrick Kavanagh Prize and Hennessy Literature Awards. She was awarded an Arts Council of Ireland literature bursary in 2004 and 2011, a Simba Gill Fellowship in 2005 and an artists' bursary from South Dublin County Council in 2007. She has published two previous poetry collections, Bar Talk, Italics Press (1999) and Trapping a Ghost, Bluechrome (2005) as well as a verse novel, In Sight of Home, Salmon Poetry (2009).